Children of John & Louisa Chittick. From Left: Elias Chittick, Edward Chittick, Grover Chittick, Rachel Chittick Morris, Howard Chittick, Herbert Chittick, and Enos Chittick.

Edward Chittick

Elmer Russell Achey (left) and Edwin Achey Jr. (right).

Edwin Achey Sr. (left) and Herbert Achey, his son (right)

Eleanor Pilcher

Eleanor Pilcher

Elizabeth Carver Bussinger

Elizabeth Shick

Elizabeth Shick

Elizabeth Shick

Viola Shick Achey and Elmer Russell Achey

Grave of Viola Shick Achey and Elmer Russell Achey

Back row, left to right: Elmer Russell Achey and Viola Shick Achey.
Front row, left to right: Freda Ludwick and an unidentified boy.

Viola Shick Achey and Elmer Russell Achey

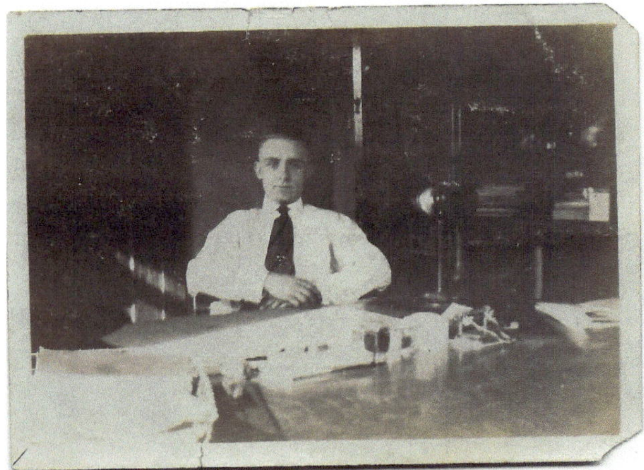

Elmer Russell Achey

Viola Shick Achey and Elmer Russell Achey

Viola Shick Achey and Elmer Russell Achey

Elmer Achey's grave, 1937

Elmer Achey's grave, 1937

Elmer Achey's grave, 1937

Elmer Russell Achey

Elmer Russell Achey

Elmer Russell Achey (left) and Helen Shick Carver (right)

From left to right: Eva Lynch and her granddaughter Ruth Back Taylor.

Eva Lynch, May 31, 1932

Warner W. and Mary Hannah (Cosner) Peters with George William Scarborough Jr.

Nona Halbe

Ruth Amy Durborow

Ruth Back Taylor

Ruth Back Taylor

Ruth Back Taylor

Ruth Back Taylor

Ruth Back Taylor

Ruth Back Taylor

Ruth Back Taylor

Timothy Eisner

Grave of Timothy Eisner

Titus Frank Carver

Grave of Titus Frank Carver

Titus Frank Carver

Titus William Carver

Titus William Carver

Titus William Carver

From left to right: Freda C. Ludwick, Mary Ellen Shick, Helen Shick Carver, an uncle, Viola Shick Achey, Sylvester Shick, and Amy Shick Trouts, about 1912

From left to right: Helen Shick Carver, Freda C. Ludwick, and Viola Shick Achey.

Earl Carver and Viola Shick Achey, May 21, 1943

Viola Shick Achey

Viola Shick Achey (left) and Helen Shick Carver (right).

Viola Shick Achey is in the top row, far right.

Viola Shick Achey (third from right) and Amy Shick Trouts (fourth from right).

Viola Shick Achey

Viola Shick Achey

Freda C. Ludwick (left) and Viola Shick Achey (right)

Viola Shick Achey

Freda C. Ludwick (left) and Viola Shick Achey (right)

Viola Shick Achey (left) and Helen Shick Carver (right)

Viola Shick Achey

Viola Shick Achey

Viola Shick Achey

Viola Shick Achey

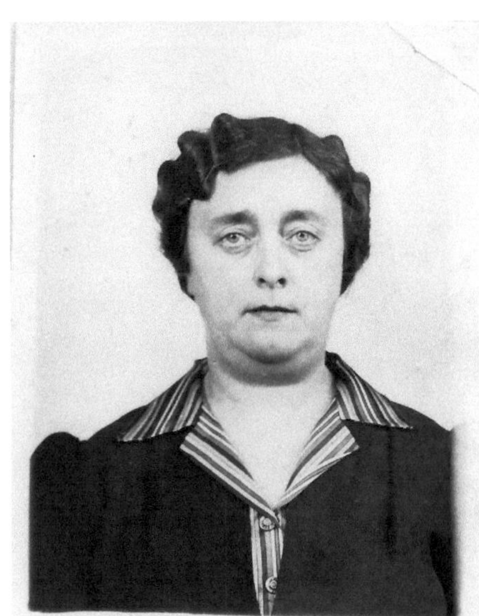

Viola Shick Achey

Freda C. Ludwick (left) and Viola Shick Achey (right)

Viola Shick Achey (right) with an unknown woman.

Amy Shick Trouts (far left) and Viola Shick Achey (far right)

Viola Shick Achey

Viola Shick Achey and Clarence Weaver

Viola Shick Achey (right) with unidentified woman

Viola Shick Achey (left) with unidentified woman

Amy Shick Trouts (left) and Viola Shick Achey (right)

Viola Shick Achey (left) with unidentified woman

Amy Shick Trouts (back row, second from right) and Viola Shick Achey (front row, right)

Viola Shick Achey (left) with unidentified woman

Walter Jack Eisner

William E. Ludwick

William Harvey Shick

Martha Selma Peters Radcliff

Catherine Shick Samsel

Russell Peter Samsel, left.

Russell Peter Samsel, right.

Mary Frances Coleman Carver Saputo

Grave of George R. Shick and Eliza Shick

Estella E. Shick

George Diehl Shick

Marie Shick 1873 died March 14th 1894
Freeland
FRENCHTOWN
EVERY
WEDNESDAY
MILFORD!
HUNTERDON CO., N. J.

Maria Shick

Madeline Trouts

Grave of Emma Carver Weidner and Lewis R. Weidner

Nona Halbe Wiggins